Christmas Presents

HOLIDAY POETRY

Christmas

An I Can Read Book™

Presents

HOLIDAY POETRY

selected by Lee Bennett Hopkins
pictures by Melanie Hall

HarperCollins*Publishers*

ACKNOWLEDGMENTS

Thanks are due to the following for use of works specially commissioned for this collection:

Sandra Gilbert Brüg for "Making Presents." Used by permission of the author, who controls all rights.

Curtis Brown, Ltd., for "Soon" and "Midnight Mass" by Rebecca Kai Dotlich; copyright © 2004 by Rebecca Kai Dotlich. "Our Tree" and "Wonder" by Lee Bennett Hopkins; copyright © 2004 by Lee Bennett Hopkins. All used by permission of Curtis Brown, Ltd.

Lillian M. Fisher for "Secrets." Used by permission of the author, who controls all rights.

Maria Fleming for "Snow Globe" and "Waiting." Used by permission of the author, who controls all rights.

Highlights for Children, Inc., for "Christmas Eve" by Stefi Weisburd; copyright © 2001 by Highlights for Children, Inc., Columbus, Ohio.

Amy Ludwig VanDerwater for "Christmas Night." Used by permission of the author, who controls all rights.

Katie McAllaster Weaver for "Colors." Used by permission of the author, who controls all rights.

Library of Congress Cataloging-in-Publication Data
Christmas presents : holiday poetry / selected by Lee Bennett Hopkins ; pictures by Melanie Hall.—1st ed.
    p. cm. — (An I can read book)
    Summary: A collection of poems by a variety of authors celebrating the various aspects of Christmas.
    ISBN 0-06-008054-X — ISBN 0-06-008055-8 (lib. bdg.)
    1. Christmas—Juvenile poetry. 2. Children's poetry, American. [1. Christmas—Poetry. 2. American Poetry—Collections.] I. Hopkins, Lee Bennett. II. Hall, Melanie W., ill. III. Series.
PS595.C48C48 2004
811.008'0334—dc22
                                                                            2003049513

1 2 3 4 5 6 7 8 9 10
❖
First Edition

To
Charles John Egita —
a
Christmas
gift
—L.B.H.

To Katya,
with love
—M.W.H.

CONTENTS

WAITING

BY MARIA FLEMING

Each day that dawns,

yawns.

Each night that falls,

crawls.

Each minute that ticks,

sticks.

And I go on waiting . . .

and waiting . . .

Waiting's the *worst*.

Because Christmas is coming

and I'm ready to BURST.

9

COLORS

BY KATIE McALLASTER WEAVER

Christmas lights string

the edge of

our roof

colors pierce

black night

air

forcing even the
biggest, brightest
stars to
stare.

SECRETS

BY LILLIAN M. FISHER

There are presents in closets,
  in cupboards,
  in drawers.

There are secrets whispered
behind closed doors.

Days are dancing hours away.

Oh, I wish Christmas

could

stay,

stay,

stay.

MAKING PRESENTS

BY SANDRA GILBERT BRÜG

First I squash them in a dish,

One banana, two banana

three banana squish.

Add the sugar, eggs and flour.

Heat it for at least an hour.

for
teacher

Smells of sweetness fill my head,

Hope she likes banana bread.

Tie it with a big, red bow—

I'm *baking* a present

    for a teacher I know.

SOON

BY REBECCA KAI DOTLICH

I am mittens

soft and red,

I am sweetest

gingerbread.

I am strings

of twinkling lights.

I am silver silent nights.

I am tinsel.

I am plums.

I am jingle bells,

tin drums.

16

I am Santa's

midnight sleigh.

Soon

I will be

Christmas Day.

OUR TREE

BY LEE BENNETT HOPKINS

We're finished

trimming.

Our tree

brims

from

limb to limb.

Underneath

the lowest branch

milk and cookies

wait

for

him.

CHRISTMAS EVE

BY STEFI WEISBURD

After tamales we walk

through Old Town

to see the luminarias,

rows of bags aglow

on streets, on snow;

lined up on the flat roofs,

like soldiers

or a choir of candles.

Imagine what the moon

sees, looking down

in the night:

a planet of people

making their own

starlight.

MIDNIGHT MASS

BY REBECCA KAI DOTLICH

Midnight now,

church bells chime

a lullaby

for Christmastime.

Like stars, small candles

string their light

from hand

    to hand

        to hand tonight—

For stable, for star,

for Wise Men we sing:

young camel, sweet lamb—

keep watch of our King.

WONDER

BY LEE BENNETT HOPKINS

Wonder

what it

was like

back then—

a mother

father

manger

Three Wise Men.

A newborn's

wailing cry

softened

by a lullaby.

Wonder.

Awe.

Joy.

Birth of

Him

Baby

Boy.

from

AWAY IN A MANGER

BY WILLIAM JAMES KIRKPATRICK

Away in a manger,

no crib for a bed.

The little Lord Jesus

lay down his sweet head.

The stars in the sky

looked down where He lay.

The little Lord Jesus

asleep on the hay.

CHRISTMAS NIGHT

BY AMY LUDWIG VANDERWATER

After all the gifts

After dinner is done

After everyone goes home

We lay by the Christmas tree—

My new book and me.

SNOW GLOBE

BY MARIA FLEMING

In here, it's always

Christmas Day,

where a tiny Santa

rides a tiny sleigh,

bringing tiny gifts

to a tiny home—

all locked inside

a plastic dome.

Shake it,

and it snows and snows,

and Christmas never

ever

goes.

Index of Authors and Titles